D1384510

ECOSYSTEMS
IN ACTION

LIFE IN A
RAIN FOREST

LIFE IN A
RAIN FOREST

ANNE WELSBACHER

Lerner Publications Company
Minneapolis

This book is dedicated to my roots and wings: my parents, Betty and Dick Welsbacher; my brother, Rick Welsbacher; and my stepdaughter, Zoë Clark.

Lerner Publications Company
A division of Lerner Publishing Group
241 First Avenue North
Minneapolis, Minnesota 55401 U.S.A.

Website address: www.lernerbooks.com

Library of Congress Cataloging-in-Publication Data

Welsbacher, Anne, 1955–.
    Life in a rain forest / by Anne Welsbacher.
        p.   cm. – (Ecosystems in action)
    Summary: Describes the ecosystems of the rain forests of Hawaii, how human activities have affected these forests, and what is being done to protect them.
        ISBN: 0–8225–4685–X (lib. bdg. : alk. paper)
        1. Rain forest ecology—Hawaii—Juvenile literature. [1. Rain forest ecology—Hawaii. 2. Rain forests—Hawaii. 3. Ecology—Hawaii.] I. Title. II. Series.
    QH198.H3 W45 2003
    577.34'09969–dc21   2002013952

Manufactured in the United States of America
1 2 3 4 5 6 – JR – 08 07 06 05 04 03

CONTENTS

INTRODUCTION
WHAT IS AN ECOSYSTEM?

An ecosystem is a community of organisms—such as trees, insects, and birds—living together within a specific physical environment that supports them. Organisms that live in a particular ecosystem are adapted to that system's environment. For example, a plant that needs a lot of water to grow, such as a fern, lives in an ecosystem where rainfall is frequent, like a rain forest. The physical environment includes water, climate, soil, air, nutrients, and energy.

WATER, CLIMATE, SOIL, AND AIR

Water can be found in the form of rainfall, puddles, or groundwater (water that is stored within cracks and crevices in rocks and soil). Water can come from various sources, such as clouds or rivers. It moves slowly, as in deep lakes, or quickly, as in hard rain. It can be warm or cold.

Climate is the average weather found in a particular location. Some environments are cold in the winter and hot in the summer. Others vary in temperature by only a few degrees from one season to the next.

Soil is composed of a variety of elements, such as decomposing leaves, volcanic ash, sand, or clay. Soil layers can be thin or thick. Air also contains various components, such as oxygen and moisture. Like water, air varies in temperature and speed of movement. Elevation—height or depth—affects water, climate, soil, and air.

These physical elements shape the nature of every individual ecosystem. For example, air moving slowly across a large expanse of ocean water will carry more moisture than air blowing across desert sands. Rising air will be warmer than falling air. Soil that is porous will hold more water or air than will dense soil.

ALL LIVING THINGS, PHYSICAL CHARACTERISTICS, AND NATURAL FORCES IN A SPECIFIC AREA
CONTRIBUTE TO THAT AREA'S ECOSYSTEM.

PRODUCERS, CONSUMERS, DECOMPOSERS

Within every ecosystem, nutrients and energy flow among primary producers, primary consumers, secondary consumers, and decomposers.

Primary producers such as plants use photosynthesis, a chemical process, to turn the sun's energy into food. They also use water and substances from the soil to produce food. Primary consumers, or herbivores, eat plants and substances produced by plants, like nectar and flowers. Secondary consumers, or carnivores, eat other animals. Bacteria and fungi are among the decomposers that break down dead plants and animals into nutrients, which go into the soil, where they are used by plants.

The cycle of energy involved in producing and consuming food is called a food chain. Within an ecosystem are various and overlapping food chains, called a food network or food web. A bird, for example, might function as both a primary consumer, eating plants, and a secondary consumer, eating insects that feed on plants.

Different types of ecosystems occur in different places. A tide pool near the shores of an island is one type of ecosystem. A patch of land near the top of a mountain on its windy side is another. Sometimes ecosystems overlap—the organisms in part of one ecosystem are very similar to those in a nearby ecosystem. Areas of overlap are called transitional areas.

RAIN FORESTS

A rain forest contains tall trees growing in a climate with abundant rainfall—more

PLANTS, SUCH AS THESE FERNS, PRODUCE THEIR OWN FOOD THROUGH PHOTOSYNTHESIS.

than 100 inches (250 centimeters) per year and sometimes up to 400 inches (1,000 centimeters) per year. Rain forests have several layers, including a canopy at the top, a shaded understory, and the floor's groundcover. Emergent trees poke up above the canopy.

Although rain forests cover only about 7 percent of the earth's surface, they support more than half the world's kinds of animals and plants. Most rain forests grow near the equator in South America, Asia, Africa, Australia, and the Pacific Islands. These forests are called tropical rain forests.

THE HAWAIIAN RAIN FOREST

The only tropical rain forests in the United States grow on several islands in the state of Hawaii. The Hawaiian rain forest grows in lowlands, on mountainsides, and in valleys.

The ʻŌlaʻa rain forest is located in Hawaiʻi Volcanoes National Park. Here, air from the ocean rises along a mountainside, forms clouds, and drops water in the form of rainfall. The soil is rich with ash from the volcanoes that formed the Hawaiian Islands. The soil nurtures groves of tall trees that form a canopy over the ground beneath them. Insects live in the bark, leaves, and roots of the trees. Birds drink nectar from the blossoms of flowering plants. Fungi break down dead plants and animals, bringing nutrients back into the soil and completing the cycle of energy.

And nearly every day, warm rain falls over the Hawaiian forest, renewing the wet environment that sustains the rain forest ecosystem.

> RAIN FORESTS HAVE SEVERAL LAYERS, INCLUDING A CANOPY AT THE TOP, A SHADED UNDERSTORY, AND THE FLOOR'S GROUNDCOVER. EMERGENT TREES POKE UP ABOVE THE CANOPY.

NORTH PACIFIC OCEAN

KAUA`I

NI`IHAU

OAHU

MOLOKA`I

LĀNA`I

MAUI

KAHO`OLAWE

HAWAI`I

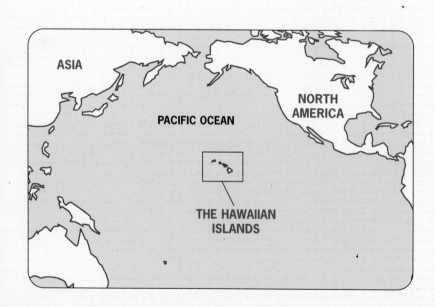

ASIA

NORTH
AMERICA

PACIFIC OCEAN

THE HAWAIIAN
ISLANDS

CHAPTER 1
THE HAWAIIAN RAIN FOREST

The Hawaiian Islands have been called the "biological crown jewels of the United States." Most of the world's types of ecosystems exist on these small islands, even though the amount of land on all of them is only 6,500 square miles (17,000 square kilometers).

Eight major islands and more than one hundred smaller ones make up the archipelago, or chain of islands, called the Hawaiian Islands. Collectively, all these islands make up the state of Hawaii.

The Hawaiian Islands extend from southeast to northwest across the north Pacific Ocean. The island of Hawai`i, also called the Big Island to differentiate it from the whole chain of islands, is at the southeastern end of the chain. To the northwest are Maui, Kaho`olawe, Lāna`i, Moloka`i, O`ahu, Kaua`i, and Ni`ihau.

The Big Island lies near the very center of the Pacific Ocean, a long way from any of the earth's continents. The continental United States sits 2,400 miles (3,900 kilometers) to its east. Japan, to its west, is 3,800 miles (6,100 kilometers) away.

The Hawaiian Islands support about 150 different ecosystems, representing nearly all

`ŌLA`A RAIN FOREST ON THE ISLAND OF HAWAI`I

the types of ecosystems found in the world. These ecosystems are categorized as either aquatic (water based), subterranean (underground), or terrestrial (land based).

The Hawaiian rain forest is in a terrestrial environment. Terrestrial ecosystems are classified by their elevation, their amount of moisture, and their dominant life-forms. A dominant plant or animal is the one that grows most commonly within an ecosystem.

Elevations on the island of Hawai`i are divided into five ranges. The coastal range includes elevations from sea level to 100 feet (30 meters) above sea level, and the lowland area ranges from 100 feet to about 3,000 feet (1,000 meters). The montane region extends from about 3,000 to 6,000 feet (1,000 to 2,000 meters). The subalpine goes from about 6,000 to 9,000 feet (2,000 to 3,000 meters), and the alpine region includes elevations more than 9,000 feet (3,000 meters) above sea level. The Hawaiian rain forest grows at elevations ranging from lowland to montane level. The rain forest is a wet environment that receives more than 100 inches (250 centimeters) of annual rainfall.

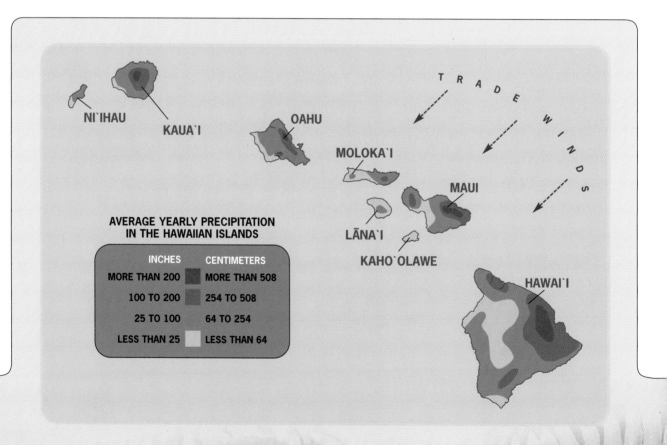

AVERAGE YEARLY PRECIPITATION
IN THE HAWAIIAN ISLANDS

INCHES		CENTIMETERS
MORE THAN 200		MORE THAN 508
100 TO 200		254 TO 508
25 TO 100		64 TO 254
LESS THAN 25		LESS THAN 64

It is dominated by trees rather than other forms of plants. Its canopy is dense in most areas, rather than predominantly open. Trees cover 60 to 100 percent of the forest.

THE RISE OF THE HAWAIIAN RAIN FOREST

The Hawaiian Islands form an archipelago that—at 2,000 miles (3,000 kilometers) long—is the largest, longest, and oldest in the world. The Hawaiian Islands are also the most geographically isolated islands in the world.

The earth's crust is made of separate solid plates, known as tectonic plates, that float on top of a hot mantle made of semisolid magma, or molten rock. The plates are made of the same material as the mantle they sit on, but they have cooled and hardened into solid rock. The Hawaiian Islands were created when hot magma beneath a plate on the bottom of the ocean broke through a weak spot, called the Hawaiian hot spot, and erupted as a volcano. Lava spewed up and cooled, forming a solid mass. Each time the volcano erupted, more lava spread a new layer over the mass. It grew higher and higher, gradually reaching above sea level and appearing as a spot of land surrounded by ocean.

The tectonic plate, shifting over the hot magma, moved slowly northwestward. Volcanic eruptions continued to create new islands in a chain. The oldest islands, at the northwestern end, began forming as early as seventy million years ago. The middle islands include O`ahu, which is four or five million years old. The youngest island at the southeastern end, the Big Island, is a mere five hundred thousand to

THE HAWAIIAN RAIN FOREST IS IN A TERRESTRIAL ENVIRONMENT. TERRESTRIAL ECOSYSTEMS ARE CLASSIFIED BY THEIR ELEVATION, THEIR AMOUNT OF MOISTURE, AND THEIR DOMINANT LIFE-FORMS.

seven hundred thousand years old. Southeast of Hawai`i, the newest member of the chain is still forming. Lō`ihi, about 0.5 mile (0.8 kilometer) below the surface of the ocean, will rise above the water to become a new island in ten thousand to twenty thousand years.

The land on these islands began as cooling, lifeless lava. Dust and ash spewed from still-erupting volcanoes and fell over the lava. Rain mixed with the dust and ash to form mud.

Eventually, plants and small animals from the mainland began to find their way to the islands. These plants and animals, or colonizers, came to the islands in various ways. Seeds were caught in the feet or feathers of birds that flew to the islands. Mud dried onto ducks' webbed feet, trapping snails that became passengers. Insects sailed to the islands trapped in floating mats of organic debris such as grasses, sticks, or leaves. Some of the arrivals did not survive the trip or lived and died without producing offspring. But others survived and reproduced. They grew into what would become a wealth of plants and animals.

VOLCANIC ASH FROM ERUPTING VOLCANOES HELPED TO FORM THE FIRST LAYERS OF SOIL ON THE HAWAIIAN ISLANDS.

More than ten thousand kinds of plants and animals live in the Hawaiian rain forest and nowhere else on earth.

Some of the first early seeds were able to sprout right on the lava rock. They grew with no soil and no nutrients except rain. Blue-green algae and other simple plant forms, such as mosses, lichens, and ferns, also appeared quickly.

These early plants dropped leaves that mixed with the mud. The decaying leaves added more nutrients to the soil. Gradually, the soil layer became thicker, and more kinds of plants were able to grow.

AFTER LAVA COOLS, SOME PLANTS ARE ABLE TO GROW DIRECTLY ON THE HARDENED SURFACE.

EVOLVING LIFE

All species, plant or animal, develop over time through a process called evolution. A species is a group of animals that share common traits—a kind of thorn for protection; sharp, curved claws capable of killing prey quickly; or a long bill that can reach into deep crevices for food. Over time, the successful traits—those that help animals in the species live and reproduce—are retained. Unsuccessful or useless traits disappear.

Sometimes species evolve into organisms whose traits have changed so much that scientists assign them a new species category. This radical evolution process is called speciation. Organisms that have gone through it are said to have speciated. If one species evolves into many new species, the process is called adaptive radiation. Hawaiian plants and animals are among the world's best examples of adaptive radiation. The species that evolved through adaptive radiation are endemic, meaning they live only in the Hawaiian Islands.

Very few colonizers made the long journey to the Hawaiian Islands. Every ten thousand years or so, another plant or animal successfully made the journey. But once a species arrived, it evolved quickly.

Because of the expanse of ocean between the nearest continent and the islands, no large predators could manage the journey. The hoary bat and the seal were the only mammals of any kind to arrive on their own. The absence of predators and the moderate climate year-round created safe, gentle conditions for growth. Defense mechanisms fell away. Plants did not need thorns for protection. Many birds and insects did not need the ability to fly. Many Hawaiian mint plants lost the scented oils that fend off plant-eating animals such as goats and sheep, because no such animals lived in Hawaiian rain forests. The energy required to evolve such defense mechanisms went instead into very fast adaptation to the living conditions of the islands.

Birds developed bills of a very specific shape to crack open a certain kind of seed. Plants blossomed with brightly colored flowers to draw more pollinating animals. Other plants changed their reproductive strategy entirely. For example, the species

HAWAIIAN MONK SEALS (MONACHUS SCHAUINSLANDI)

Hibiscus, which on the mainland is pollinated by moths, evolved into the endemic genus *Hibiscadelphus* (hau kuahiwi), a group of species that are pollinated by birds.

Some species coevolved, developing features that were useful to both. For example, some lobelia plants developed long, narrow, tubelike flowers. At the same time, a species of Hawaiian honeycreeper developed a long, curved beak that fits precisely into the flowers of the lobelias.

Through adaptive radiation, the first few creatures that colonized the islands speciated quickly into an enormous number of new species. The number of colonizing plants was about 275. These evolved into nearly 1,000 species of flowering plants. Between 350 and 400 insect species evolved to become as many as 10,000. About 20 bird species became about 80.

The land itself evolved quickly, as well. Lifeless lava became soils of deep ash and rich particles of humus made of decomposed plants and animals. Warm temperatures quickened the process. The ash soils that built the land, supporting plants that were specially suited to live in it, help support the rain forests that still grow on the islands.

(ABOVE) **VOLCANIC ASH AND DECAYING PLANTS AND ANIMALS BECAME A LAYER OF FERTILE SOIL.**

(LEFT) **SOME BIRDS, SUCH AS THE ʻIʻIWI, DEVELOPED SPECIALIZED BEAKS FOR FEEDING FROM FLOWERS.**

HAWAIIAN HONEYCREEPERS: ADAPTIVE RADIATION IN FLIGHT

Hawaiian honeycreepers exist nowhere else on earth. They evolved from a finchlike colonizer, adapting to the specific environment and diet available to them in the Hawaiian Islands. Among about 40 species of honeycreeper are the Maui parrotbill, which lives in the rain forest on Maui, and the i`iwi and `apapane, which both live on Hawai`i.

The Maui Parrotbill
(Pseudonestor xanthophrys)

The Maui parrotbill is named for its location, the rain forests of Maui, and for its powerful bill.

The bill resembles a parrot's in strength as well as in appearance. Its large, hooked bill can pry bark off a koa tree or break understory twigs in search of beetles and other food. The jaws of this small bird are much stronger than those of most birds its size. They can slice and wrench at the same time.

The parrotbill is about 5.5 inches (14 centimeters) long, with a short tail. Its body is olive green and its chest bright yellow. Over its eyes is a bright yellow band. Its wing and tail feathers are brown with an olive-green border.

The Maui parrotbill lives and forages in koa trees and `ōhi`as. It eats beetles and their larvae. To forage, it clings to the underside of a branch, stretches its neck up, and grabs hold of a small twig or branch with its jaw. It wrenches and twists the twig, which is made of very hard wood, until it breaks apart. Then it uses its upper bill and tongue to extract beetle larvae.

The Maui parrotbill emits a short, vigorous trill, sometimes while flying. The call is a descending "cheer-cheer-cheer."

Maui parrotbills build cup-shaped nests high in the canopy in the forks of `ōhi`a trees. The nests are made of lichen held together with small twigs. The birds lay only one egg. Newly hatched nestlings grow to fledglings in about twenty days. At this age, they can leave the nest and fly easily from tree to tree. The fledglings leave the nest in less than one day but stay in the vicinity with their parents for five to eight months before striking out on their own.

The `Ī`iwi (*Vestiaria coccinea*)

The `ī`iwi is a brilliant orange-red bird with orange legs and black wings and tail. A few white features border the wings where they meet the body. The bird is 5.5 inches (14 centimeters) long, with a short tail and short wings. Its peach-colored bill is very long and curved. Shaped by evolution over thousands of years, it perfectly matches the shape of tubular flowers in the lobelioid group of flowering plants, which includes the `ōhā. Its bill coevolved with these plants.

The `ī`iwi has a rusty, discordant singing voice. It also emits loud, clear whistles. It can mimic other birds. When it flies, its flapping wings are noisy. It can be seen and heard even when high in `ōhi`a trees.

The `ī`iwi bird eats the nectar of lobelioid plants and of `ōhi`a flowers. It feeds in both the high treetops of the upper canopy and in understory shrubs. It is a powerful flier and migrates from one area of the forest to another, following flowering seasons in search of food. To eat, it perches on a twig near the flower. It swings upside down and twists its body to bring its head up under the flower. It slips its beak completely into the long flower, sips for a few seconds, and flies quickly to the next flower to repeat its action. The `ī`iwi also eats caterpillars and spiders. It hunts for them with quick, gliding flights among the leaves of trees.

`I`iwi birds build cup-shaped nests in tall `ōhi`a trees. They lay one to three eggs, which they incubate for two weeks. Fledglings leave the nest three weeks after hatching. The young birds are yellow green with short, brownish green bills. As they grow, their bills curve and lengthen. Both bills and plumage gradually change to the striking colors of the adult birds.

The `Apapane (*Himatione sanguinea*)

The `apapane is the most common species of honeycreeper. Its body is almost solid crimson red, except for fluffy white feathers under its tail. Its wings and tail are black. The bird often cocks them up at a 45-degree angle when foraging for food or, if male, courting. It is 5.25 inches (13 centimeters) long. The `apapane moves quickly and frequently among the high branches of the `ōhi`a tree in search of food. It has a black, slightly curved bill that is shorter than the bill of the `i`iwi.

`Apapane sing pleasant, complex songs. Their calls sound like whistles, trills, buzzing, clucking, or squawking. Their songs are distinct and differ from island to island. The birds on each island have their own dialects. As `apapane birds fly, their wings produce a whirring sound that can easily be heard at long distances. `Apapane fly farther than other honeycreepers, as high as 7,000 feet (2,000 meters) up a mountain or several hundred feet above the top canopy of the forest.

`Apapane eat caterpillars and spiders and drink the nectar of `ōhi`a blossoms. They also drink from flowering koa trees. They follow flowering seasons from one `ōhi`a tree to the next and pollinate the flowers as they move among them. They travel widely in search of food.

`Apapane build nests high in the thin branches of `ōhi`a trees, on smaller `ōhi`a trees, or in tree-fern fronds. Nests are cup shaped. They lay two to four eggs, which they incubate for about two weeks. Nestlings grow for two and one-half weeks. Then they are able to fly from tree to tree.

THE ʻŌLAʻA FOREST

The Hawaiian rain forest grows on Hawaiʻi, Maui, Kauaʻi, Molokaʻi, and Oʻahu. About 350,000 acres (140,000 hectares) of pristine rain forest grows on the Big Island. About the same amount grows on Maui, Kauaʻi, Oʻahu, and Molokaʻi combined.

The ʻŌlaʻa rain forest lies in Hawaiʻi Volcanoes National Park, on the island of Hawaiʻi. It is one of the most pristine tracts of rain forest in the Hawaiian Islands. It is located 19 degrees north of the equator. The ʻŌlaʻa rain forest is an old forest by Hawaiian standards, supported by deep ash soils that have been allowed to develop and mature.

Hawaiʻi Volcanoes National Park is home to two active volcanoes, Mauna Loa and Mauna Kīlauea. At 13,680 feet (4,170 meters) high, Mauna Loa is the largest volcanic mass in the world. Mauna Kīlauea, rising 4,090 feet (1,247 meters) above sea level, flanks Mauna Loa's eastern slope. From elevations of about 1,000 feet (300 meters) to about 4,000 feet (over 1,000 meters), rain forests grow

along Mauna Kīlauea's eastern side. Among them is the 9,000-acre (4,000-hectare) ʻŌlaʻa forest, which rests along a gently sloping grade from elevations of about 3,500 to 5,500 feet (1,100 to 1,700 meters). Kīlauea volcano is still active. During the past one thousand years, it has dumped lava over more than 90 percent of its surface.

Rain falls almost every day in the ʻŌlaʻa forest. Wet trade winds gather moisture from the sea, rise up the side of the mountain, and cool. These cooler winds become clouds. Beads of water form around particles in the air until they become so heavy that they turn to rain, dumping more than 100 inches (250 centimeters) of rain annually onto the forest. Year-round temperatures in ʻŌlaʻa average between 50 and 75 degrees Fahrenheit (10 to 24 degrees Celsius).

Clouds or fog, fed by northeastern trade winds from the ocean, frequently envelop the ʻŌlaʻa forest. The air is cool and damp under the closed, shady canopy of the forest. In many places, the ground is heavy, wet, and muddy. Walking through the foliage can be difficult. But in other areas, the path is clear.

The Hawaiian rain forests grow in layers. They can be divided by height into the top canopy, which includes emergent trees and a subcanopy level; the understory; and the groundcover. Many plants and animals live in more than one layer, and many plants grow to different heights depending on the amount of sunshine they receive. So although the forest has distinct layers, many of the plants and animals are not so easily divided. They stretch and wind their ways through many layers within the `Ōla`a forest. In other places within the Hawaiian rain forest—on Maui or O`ahu, for example—these same plants and animals might differ in eating habits, size, the height to which they grow, or other ways, depending on those areas' physical conditions.

In `Ōla`a, the treetops form a dense canopy 30 feet (10 meters) or higher above the ground. One large tree, the

THE ISLAND OF HAWAI`I

PACIFIC OCEAN

MAUNA LOA

X

`ŌLA`A RAIN FOREST

MAUNA KĪLAUEA
X

HAWAI`I VOLCANOES NATIONAL PARK

`ōhi`a, dominates this layer. Broad, tall tree ferns and smaller trees form a subcanopy, or secondary tree layer, just below the canopy. The tree ferns here can reach to nearly 20 feet (6 meters).

Beneath this layer grow shrubs, tree saplings, and nearly fifty different species of ferns. These plants form the understory layer of the rain forest. This layer is dark, shaded from the sun by the dense top canopy. Along with the shade-loving plants that grow in the understory are spiders and songbirds, as well as caterpillars, damselflies, and other insects.

Epiphytes snake their way around the trunks of the canopy and understory's trees and ferns, often growing as tall as their host plants. Epiphytes are plants that grow on other plants but are not dependent on them for sustenance. They get the moisture and nutrients they need from the air and rain. Because they do not grow from soil, they are sometimes called "air plants." Vines cling to the trees as well. High above the top canopy, a few emergent palms stretch up through the shady forest rooftop into the warm, steady sunshine above the Hawaiian rain forest.

The rain forest's groundcover is its bottom layer. Small ferns, shrubs, herbs (nonwoody, seed-producing plants), and saplings grow in soil covered with decomposing leaves and fern fronds. Mosses and liverworts cover the tree trunks. Pools of water collect in the pockets of leaves. In and around these pools live damselflies and snails.

A DIFFERENT SORT OF RAIN FOREST

The Hawaiian rain forest differs from rain forests in other places around the world. For example, dozens of different kinds of trees populate the canopy of South American rain forests. But only one or two trees dominate the Hawaiian rain forest canopy. Hawaiian vines, which grow to about 20 feet (6 meters), are much smaller than the South American rain forest's massive vines, which can grow to 200 feet (60 meters) or more. The Hawaiian islands' isolation in the

Pacific Ocean and their climate are factors in these differences.

Because of the archipelago's isolation in the Pacific Ocean, life evolved differently on its islands than it did on large continental landmasses like South America and Asia. Fewer genes from fewer types of plants and animals could flow to the islands. The islands are also isolated from one another, so on each island, life evolved differently.

Other islands evolved in similar ways, beginning as small areas of land built up from volcanic eruptions on the ocean floor. Their isolation from large bodies of land led to unique evolution of life. On the Galápagos Islands, 600 miles (1,000 kilometers) west of South America, and on Madagascar, off the east coast of Africa, a huge diversity of plants and animals evolved. Flightless birds evolved on New Zealand, which lies northwest of Australia. Island species include many that are much larger (gigantism) or smaller (dwarfism) than similar species on large continents.

In the Hawaiian Islands, different ecosystems on individual islands also are isolated. Mountains are isolated from other mountains and valleys from other valleys. Another kind of isolation occurs in kīpukas, which are distinctly Hawaiian creations. Kīpukas are older sections of lava on which vegetation has grown. New volcanic eruptions often spew fresh lava over the vegetation, burying it. But sometimes the lava flows around older, vegetated areas, leaving them uncovered. More mature stands of trees and other organisms grow on these kīpukas, which become isolated from other kīpukas.

As a result of this isolation, there is less diversity of plants and animals in the Hawaiian rain forests than can be found in continental rain forests. Sometimes individual species occupy very small areas in the Hawaiian rain forest. The entire territory of certain Hawaiian rain forest tree snails is only one tree.

The Hawaiian islands' climate differs from area to area throughout the island chain. Sometimes it differs between areas that are very small distances apart. Rainfall, in particular, varies widely. It averages between 25 and 30 inches

(63 to 76 centimeters) annually. But rainfall on the islands can be up to fifteen times as much in some places and only one-third as much in others. The differences are caused by the flow of moist trade winds moving northeastward over the steep, varied island terrain.

The windward side of a mountain at elevations of 3,000 to 6,000 feet (1,000 to 2,000 meters) might receive 400 inches (1,000 centimeters) or more of rain annually, because trade winds bring moisture from the ocean. But only a few miles away, on the other side of the same mountain at the same elevation, rainfall might be as low as 10 inches (25 centimeters) a year because none of the moist winds reach that side of the mountain. Climate also differs at higher and lower elevations of the same mountain.

As a result, many very different ecosystems exist side by side in the Hawaiian Islands, sometimes very close to one another. So seeds or spores have a good chance of being distributed to completely different ecosystems. This can lead to highly random genetic variations as

ON THE HAWAIIAN ISLANDS, MANY ECOSYSTEMS EXIST CLOSE TO ONE ANOTHER.

plants evolve and adapt to their new environments. This is much less likely to happen in large continental rain forests, where a seed would have to travel a long distance to enter a different ecosystem.

UNUSUAL PLANTS AND ANIMALS

Entire groups of plants and animals that thrive in continental rain forests, such as figs and ants, do not live in the Hawaiian rain forest. They could not make the long journey. Or, in the case of some plants, seeds that reached the islands successfully grew into plants that were unable to be pollinated. For example, a specific species of wasp pollinates a specific species of fig. Unless the wasp had arrived on the island by the time the fig was flowering—highly unlikely because of the distance of the island from the mainland—the fig would fail to reproduce.

Individual groups of plants and animals in the Hawaiian rain forest diversified. They lost natural defenses, such as thorns, stinging hairs, or poisons, because no large herbivores or predators evolved on the islands. Some plants grew to be unusually large. For example, outside of the Hawaiian Islands, most lobelia are small herbs, only a few inches high. But in the Hawaiian rain forest, lobelia can grow to 13 feet (4 meters) high. Species also changed how they reproduced. For example, plants that had been pollinated by insects evolved to become capable of being pollinated by birds.

Sometimes colonizing plants and animals evolved in so many different ways—and so rapidly—that they became a large number of entirely new species. For example, the one finchlike bird that colonized the islands evolved into the forty different species of birds known collectively as Hawaiian honeycreepers.

CHAPTER 2
THE FOREST CANOPY

The top canopy of the `Ōla`a rain forest reaches 30 feet or higher (more than 10 meters). In many areas, the forest is a "closed canopy" forest. Its top canopy trees grow closely together, shutting off sunshine and shading the layers below.

In addition to providing shade for groundcover plants and animals, the trees and plants above the ground store water in their leaves, branches, trunks, and roots. Small animals retrieve this water by chewing on the leaves or bark.

TOP TREE

Dominating the `Ōla`a rain forest canopy is the `ōhi`a tree, the most abundant endemic tree in the Hawaiian Islands. The tree is also called `ōhi`a lehua.

Lehua refers to its large, usually bright red, pompom–shaped blossoms. The `ōhi`a has very dense, hard wood. Its bark is dark gray, and its branches are twisted and gnarled. Its foliage is deep green. In the `Ōla`a forest, it grows to 30 to 50 feet (9 to15 meters) or higher. Its thin branches form a twisted rooftop to the forest ecosystem. The `ōhi`a can also grow epiphytically, sprouting from logs, trunks, or branches of other trees.

The `ōhi`a was one of the first colonizers of the Hawaiian Islands. Soon after simple plants like ferns

> **IN MANY AREAS, THE FOREST IS A "CLOSED CANOPY" FOREST. ITS TOP CANOPY TREES GROW CLOSELY TOGETHER, SHUTTING OFF SUNSHINE AND SHADING THE LAYERS BELOW.**

and algae grew, the hardy tree took root on nothing more than lava. It turned sunlight and water into nutrients that fed its growth and began the development of the forest that it dominates.

JUST BELOW AND PEEKING ABOVE

The `ōlapa, a medium-sized tree with bright yellow-green, serrated-edged leaves, grows abundantly in the subcanopy of the `Ōla`a forest. Like the `ōhi`a tree, it can grow as an epiphyte as well as a tree. Sometimes an epiphytic `ōlapa grows to 30 feet (9 meters) or higher, twisted around the trunk of a tall `ōhi`a tree. In some areas, the `ōlapa and `ōhi`a are intertwined closely. It can be difficult to tell which plant is the host plant, growing from the ground, and which is the plant growing epiphytically on the other.

The kawa`u, also called Hawaiian holly, is common in the forest subcanopy. Supported by the old soils of the `Ōla`a forest, it sometimes stretches

`ŌLAPA TREES (CHEIRODENDRON TRIGYNUM) CAN GROW EPIPHYTICALLY ON OTHER TREES. HERE, AN `ŌLAPA IS SANDWICHED BETWEEN TWO `ŌHI`A TREES (METROSIDEROS POLYMORPHA).

(TOP) **HAWAIIAN HOLLY** *(ILEX ANOMALA)*

(BOTTOM) **LOULU FAN PALM**
(PRITCHARDIA BECCARIANA)

into the upper canopy, reaching as high as 60 feet (20 meters). Its leaves, like those of other holly family plants, are shiny and dark green, oval-shaped and smooth. The kawa`u bears flowers that grow in clusters. The female plants produce small round fruits with purple flesh.

Emerging high above the roof of the `Ōla`a canopy are loulu fan palms. Their bright green leaves are 3 feet (1 meter) wide or wider and point up rigidly. When the leaves die, they droop down but stay on the branches for a while, rustling loudly in the wind. Loulu flowers become fruits that grow in clusters. The fruits are eaten by insects, such as the fruit moth.

Here and there, koa trees grow just beneath or alongside `ōhi`a trees. In one area of the forest, the koa dominates the forest, emerging above the slower-growing `ōhi`a. The koa is home to many native and endemic invertebrates, (animals that are usually soft-bodied and have an external skeleton instead of a backbone).

THE KOA TREE
(Acacia koa)

The koa tree is prominent in many Hawaiian forests and lives on most of the islands in the archipelago. It thrives in many ecosystems, including dry, moderately moist, and wet forests, and at elevations between sea level and 7,000 feet (2,000 meters).

In the `Ōla`a forest, the koa grows in only one remote stand. In some Hawaiian rain forest areas, it is a keystone species: it plays a crucial role in the ecosystem in which it lives. A keystone species is any species that is very important to the survival of other species living within its ecosystem. If a keystone species were to disappear, other living parts of its ecosystem would die. The name "keystone" comes from a building term. The keystone is the key block, or stone, in an arch that holds all the other parts together.

A STAND OF KOA TREES

The koa is a fast-growing tree that can reach a height of nearly 100 feet (30 meters) in areas where the soils are deep ash. Its trunk can grow more than 20 feet (6 meters) in circumference, and the branches of its crown can spread to 125 feet (38 meters) or more. In thinner soils, the koa is shorter but develops more branches.

A young koa's bark is gray and smooth, and it grows soft, wide leaflets in bundles. These feathery leaves, with their broad surface area, can gather sunlight even in shaded conditions. Because as saplings koa trees grow on the shaded forest floor where little sunlight breaks through, this ability helps the koa tree grow. As the koa ages, its bark darkens to brown and becomes rough and furrowed. Instead of leaves, it begins to grow thin, curved leaf stalks called phyllodes. The phyllodes can store and retain large amounts of water, a good defense against periods of drought. The koa also is able to capture nitrogen, a nutrient, directly from the air. Nitrogen is essential to all plants and animals. To enter a plant, nitrogen usually must be transformed through a process in which it mixes with oxygen or hydrogen. This is often done by bacteria, or, in some cases, by algae or even lightning. The koa can take in nitrogen without going through this process.

KOA PHYLLODES

The koa is host to many plants and animals. `Ohi`a trees grow epiphytically up its massive trunk. Near its base, `ōlapa trees develop on the thick roots that run along the ground. Ferns, mosses, lichens, and fungi cover parts of its trunk. Shuttlecock ferns and hairy stag's tongue creep along its branches.

Smaller finger ferns, molds, and fungi fill crannies between the furrows in its bark and spaces near its roots. Koa bugs and moths, as well as yellow-faced bees, live in crevices in its bark. The koa beetle, a large red, white, and black insect, lives on the trunk and branches of the koa, especially on dying or fallen trees. The larvae of wood-boring beetles, nestled into the tree between its wood and its bark, provide food for native birds of the forest. `Apapane, `ōma`o, and `elepaio dig the larvae out of the tree with their beaks.

KOA BUG *(COLEOTICHUS BLACKBURNIAE)*

The koa continues to host animals and plants long after it has died. Due to its hardness, koa wood decays more slowly than the wood of most trees. Some koa logs have lain on the ground for six hundred years.

SONGBIRDS OF THE TREETOPS

Most of the birds of the Hawaiian rain forest live in the canopy. The `elepaio is a small brown bird with dark brown and white streaks on its head, wings, and rump. It often holds its tail cocked up stiffly at a sharp angle. It flies from branch to branch of the koa, moving back and forth in short spurts, seeking insects in the koa's foliage.

The `elepaio is named after its song. It whistles "ele-PAIO" or chatters rapidly. It weaves small, cup-shaped nests in the branches of the koa tree. The nests are built of grasses, lichens, and roots. Holding them together are spiderwebs, which the `elepaio gathers by flying into a web and catching it in its beak.

High in the `ōhi`a treetops, the song of the `apapane can be heard year-round. This crimson red honeycreeper flies long distances at high altitudes and makes its nest in `ōhi`a trees at the crown of the forest. The `apapane is drawn to the `ōhi`a for its blossoms, or lehua. Lehua flowers bear sweet nectar and fruit that the `apapane drinks and eats.

Also drawn to the blossoms of the `ōhi`a is the brightly colored `i`iwi bird, another kind of honeycreeper. The `i`iwi nests in the branches of the `ōhi`a tree. The noisy bird's harsh, loud song can be heard even from high in the treetops.

Many other birds live in other rain forest areas on the Big Island, sometimes at somewhat higher altitudes than the `Ōla`a forest. The `akiapola`au, another kind of honeycreeper, has a highly specialized bill. Its two mandibles (the upper and lower halves of the bill) perform two different functions. The `akiapola`au's short, strong lower mandible chisels into or hammers the bark, like a woodpecker. Its upper mandible, curved and long, can pry insects out of bark. The bird uses both mandibles to pick up food.

The male `akepa is bright red orange, while the female is greenish yellow. The `akepa uses its short, cone-shaped bill to pry open the buds of `ōhi`a flowers and the pods of large seeds in search of spiders and insects. It is one of the most active of the honeycreepers, foraging high in `ōhi`a trees for insects.

CHAPTER 3
THE UNDERSTORY

The understory of the `Ōla`a forest is shady and cool, but many kinds of plants and animals thrive in this layer. A diverse array of trees, large shrubs, and soft, thick tree ferns share the layer with songbirds and arthropods. An arthropod is an invertebrate with an exoskeleton—a hard, crusty outer layer—instead of a skeleton inside its body. Arthropods' bodies are made up of several parts joined together.

Arachnids (such as spiders and mites), insects, and crustaceans (such as crabs and shrimps) are all arthropods.

The understory ranges in height from about 20 to 40 feet (6 to 12 meters). There is more tree diversity in the understory layer than in the canopy. While one or two trees dominate the upper canopy, as many as ten different species can be found in the understory layers.

TREE FERNS ARE AN IMPORTANT PART OF THE UNDERSTORY.

VARIETY OF TREES AND FERNS

Smaller `ōlapa trees and kāwa`u plants, prominent in the rain forest canopy, grow in the understory as well. Sharing the secondary canopy and the understory are pilo trees. A member of the coffee family, the pilo grows up to 20 feet (6 meters) tall. At the base of its long, narrow, curved leaves grow reddish fruits that contain seeds resembling coffee beans. The tree itself has thin, smooth, pale gray bark. Its branches stretch to varying heights. The tips of the tree's branches and its young leaves are covered with soft, thick hairs.

The fruits of the pilo, the kāwa`u, and especially the `ōlapa tree are sought after by the `ōma`o bird, or Hawaiian thrush. It also eats seeds, insects, and caterpillars. The `ōma`o has many kinds of calls. Some are whispering songs; some sound like slurred flute notes; others are loud and shrill, like a whistle. The `ōma`o often forages in the understory of the forest but also flies to the higher canopy, where it sits singing without moving. The `ōma`o builds nests in the cavities of trees, at the bases of living or dead fronds of tree ferns, or in cracks in rocks. It builds with mosses, bits of roots, and strips of bark.

The hāpu`u pulu is the most common of various hāpu`u, or Hawaiian tree ferns, that crowd the Hawaiian rain forest's subcanopy as well as its understory. The hāpu`u pulu has large, wide, arcing fronds that stretch out in a fan shape. Its trunk is covered with orange, silky hairs. Small fiddleheads—young fern fronds—sprout up from the trunk at the base of its larger fronds. The hāpu`u pulu grows

> **A MEMBER OF THE COFFEE FAMILY, THE PILO GROWS UP TO 20 FEET (6 METERS) TALL. AT THE BASE OF ITS LONG, NARROW, CURVED LEAVES GROW REDDISH FRUITS THAT CONTAIN SEEDS RESEMBLING COFFEE BEANS.**

quickly to 20 feet (6 meters), forming a layer beneath the `ōhi`a canopy that shades the layers below. Growing amid the hāpu`u pulu are related species, the hāpu`u i`i and the less common meu. The meu retains fronds that have died. They hang down from the top of its trunk like a skirt, similar to the hanging dead leaves of the loulu fan palms that emerge above the forest canopy.

The shrub `ōhā, one of a group of shrubs and small trees known as lobelioids, grows freely on the windward side of Volcanoes National Park. Its brittle branches arch up and out like a candelabra and can grow to 10 feet (3 meters) or more. The pink, green, purple, or white petals of its flowers curl out and under, forming a deep, narrow opening. In `Ōla`a, the `ōhā usually grows epiphytically.

The `ōhelo kaulā`au, or tree `ōhelo, is a tall, deciduous shrub. In the winter, its thin, bright green leaves turn red or yellow and then fall off. Deciduous trees are common in parts of North America but are rare in the Hawaiian Islands. `Ōhelo kaulā`au bears berries related to, but tarter than, cranberries and blueberries.

(TOP) **HĀPU`U PULU** *(CIBOTIUM GLAUCUM)*

(BOTTOM) **HĀPU`U I`I** *(CIBOTIUM MENZIESII)*

The largest edible fruit in the forest grows on the ʻākala, or Hawaiian raspberry. Its stems can be smooth or prickly, and its leaves are covered with soft hairs. The flowers are dark pink, with yellow stamens clustered in their centers. They bear large red or purple fruit. Unlike many berry plants, the ʻākala's branches have no defensive thorns to protect its tart fruit.

Pāpala kēpau is a shrub or tree common in the ʻŌlaʻa understory. It grows up to 20 feet (6 meters) tall. Its flowers produce capsules covered with a sticky substance. This gluey matter can trap insects, which draw birds to the plant. They sometimes become trapped in the sticky glue as well. The fruit of the pāpala kēpau also sticks to the feathers of birds. Seeds from the fruit are dispersed when the birds fly to other areas.

Maile is a large, climbing, woody liana, or vine, with a milky, strong-smelling sap. In shady parts of the forest, it twines along trees and tree ferns and can grow to 20 feet (6 meters) or higher. In sunny spots, maile grows as a wide, full shrub. Often many maile plants grow close together, forming a thicket.

(TOP) **HAWAIIAN RASPBERRY** *(RUBUS HAWAIENSIS)*

(BOTTOM) **MAILE** *(ALYXIA OLIVIFORMIS)*

ARTHROPODS

Thousands of species of arthropods live in the Hawaiian rain forest. In the understory, flies, leafhoppers, and spiders are among the arthropods found in abundance.

Almost one-third of the world's species of pomace flies live in the Hawaiian archipelago. Pomace flies are in a family apart from that of true fruit flies. They eat pomace, the pulp of fruit. They also eat rotting fruit and leaves, fermenting tree sap, and fungi. About eight hundred different species of pomace flies living in the islands evolved from just one or two colonizing species—one of the more spectacular examples of Hawaiian speciation. Many have ornate patterns of color on their wings and bodies. About one hundred different species grow to huge proportions. Wingspans of nearly 1 inch (3 centimeters)—three times the size of normal flies—are not uncommon. Their large size may help individuals within a species recognize each other quickly.

One kind of pomace fly exhibits an elaborate mating behavior not seen in any other arthropods. Males establish breeding territories, called "leks." Females are drawn to the leks by pheromones, chemical substances that stimulate sexual or other behavior. When no females are present, males butt heads and use their wings to wrestle with each other. But when the females arrive, the males begin to perform ritual mating dances. They stroke and touch the females and release pheromones. They also flutter their wings and buzz to accompany their dances.

POMACE FLY (DROSOPHILA)

PREDACEOUS CATERPILLARS
(Eupithecia)

Predaceous (predatory) caterpillars are unique to the Hawaiian Islands. Most caterpillars consume the leaves of plants. These "ambush predators" attack and eat insects—some larger than themselves—that crawl within their reach.

A number of species of predaceous caterpillars are included in the *Eupithecia* genus, which is part of the inchworm family. These 1-inch-long (3-centimeter-long), thin inchworms are gray, brown, or green. They resemble the twigs or edges of leaves to which they cling. Green caterpillars sit on leaves or ferns. Brown ones perch on twigs. Some caterpillars have a mosslike appearance and sit on tree trunks covered with moss. The caterpillars' camouflaged coloring, texture, and shape protect them from their own enemies, birds.

THERE ARE A NUMBER OF SPECIES OF PREDACEOUS CATERPILLARS. SOME HAVE NOT YET BEEN NAMED. THIS ONE, WHICH HAS A SPINY BACK, IS A NEW DISCOVERY.

Camouflage also helps the caterpillars sit unnoticed by other insects. A caterpillar anchors itself onto a leaf using its rear prolegs and waits, motionless. One species even carves a notch in a leaf and backs into the notch for a more inconspicuous ambush spot. When sensory bristles on the rear of the caterpillar are touched by a fly, spider, cricket, or wasp, the caterpillar takes one-tenth of one second to snatch its prey with the claws on its front legs and to begin to devour it alive.

The Hawaiian predaceous caterpillar's ability to catch and consume small animals was discovered in 1972. No caterpillar anywhere else in the world is known to hunt other insects. It is one of many examples of adaptive radiation in this isolated island chain.

Predaceous caterpillars live in the vegetation of very wet areas in the Hawaiian rain forest. They live in the lehua blossoms of `ōhi`a trees or on fern fronds. Because they do not eat plants, they are not dependent on any specific kind of plant.

The caterpillars grow into adult moths that also are well camouflaged by green or brown coloring. Female moths lay about one hundred eggs that hatch into caterpillars in about two weeks. The caterpillars molt (shed their skins) four times as they grow. After the fourth molt, the caterpillar builds a cocoon and stays inside it for three weeks. It emerges as an adult moth. The adult moths drink the nectar of flowers and the juices of rotting fruit. They do not live more than a few days.

Eventually, the female pomace flies choose partners to mate with. When the population of these flies is dense and more males are available, the females are slower to select a partner than they are when few male flies are available.

Of the many species of dragonflies and damselflies in the Hawaiian Islands, two dragonfly species live in Hawai`i Volcanoes National Park. One of them, the giant pinao, is the largest insect in the United States, with a wingspan as wide as 6 inches (15 centimeters). Dragonflies and damselflies have large compound eyes, movable heads, long wings, and long legs that can grasp insects. They capture insects while flying. They live and lay eggs near water—sometimes near the tiny bit of water to be found captured in the space between a leaf and its stem. Young, developing dragonflies and damselflies, called naiads, eat mosquito larvae and other water insects.

GIANT PINAO (ANAX STRENUUS)

CHAPTER 4
THE GROUNDCOVER

The groundcover of the Hawaiian rain forest is varied. It includes the soil from which trees and plants grow and fallen chunks of branches and trees that lie on the ground. Forest litter—made of leaves, small pieces of branches, and fern fronds that have blown or fallen to the ground—also make up the groundcover. Occupying the groundcover are ground and tree snails, arthropods like beetles and spiders, and a wide variety of plants.

THE FLOOR OF THE `ŌLA`A RAIN FOREST IS MADE OF LAVA THAT ERUPTED FROM THE NEARBY VOLCANO MAUNA KĪLAUEA AND THEN COOLED AND HARDENED. LAVA IS PERMEABLE AND POROUS—IT CAN ABSORB AND HOLD LARGE AMOUNTS OF GROUNDWATER.

VOLCANIC SOIL
The floor of the `Ōla`a rain forest is made of lava that erupted from the nearby volcano Mauna Kīlauea and then cooled and hardened. Lava is permeable and porous—it can absorb and hold large amounts of groundwater.

A layer of organic soil, mixed with volcanic ash, covers the lava. The soil layer is between 6 inches (15 centimeters) and 3 feet (1 meter) thick. The soil is created when arthropods and microbes (very small living organisms) decompose organic materials such as pieces of dead plants and forest litter. Warm, moist climates, like that of the `Ōla`a forest, speed this process of decay.

The decaying material releases nutrients that help feed new plants.

Volcanic ash mixed into the soil also provides nutrients for growing plants. The decay process results in rich humus. Humus can hold large quantities of water and air, both of which are absorbed by plants' roots.

GROUNDCOVER

Topping the soil layer is a thick layer of leaves and fronds that are beginning to decompose into the soil. Arthropods such as crickets live in the leaf litter, feasting on dead plants and insects and helping to break them down.

Logs and chunks of branches that have broken from `ōhi`a and koa trees litter the floor of the forest. The wood of these trees is very hard and dense, so large logs decay much more slowly than those found in other rain forests. `Ōhi`a tree snags—some of them huge—rise out of the forest floor. A snag is a tree that has died but is still upright. Many animals and plants live in and on snags. Snails and insects nestle between the peeling bark and the wood.

The Hawaiian Islands have more than one thousand endemic species of beetles,

THE GROUNDCOVER LAYER IN `ŌLA`A IS CHARACTERIZED BY MOSSES, HERBS, AND FERNS.

including sixteen species of the *Plagithmysus* genus that live in Volcanoes National Park. The larvae of beetles bore into both living and dead rain forest trees, shrubs, and vines, such as the koa, the `ōhi`a, and the woody alani plant.

Both land snails and tree snails live in the Hawaiian rain forest. The many kinds of Hawaiian tree snails vary in size and appearance, but most of the tree snails of the `Ōla`a rain forest are smaller than 1 inch (3 centimeters), with paper-thin shells. They lay eggs on leaves. The eggs are surrounded by a layer of mucus that protects them from moisture.

A snail breathes air through a cavity between the shell and the mantle, the soft skin covering the upper part of the snail's body. Glands in a snail's body produce slime that is released onto the ground and provides a means for movement. The snail slides along the slime by contracting and releasing a large muscle called a "stomach foot." Snails thrive in damp, shaded places. They eat rotting plants and animals, scraping up particles with their radula, a large tooth-covered tongue. In turn, snails provide food for forest birds.

(ABOVE) **SNAGS MAKE HOMES FOR MANY LIFE-FORMS, SUCH AS THIS FUNGUS.**

(RIGHT) **SOME SNAGS TOWER ABOVE THE CANOPY.**

O`AHU TREE SNAILS (Achatinella)

O`AHU TREE SNAIL SHELLS

Millions of years ago, a few small land snails arrived in the Hawaiian Islands, trapped in the muddy webbed feet of water birds or perhaps blown by the wind. They slowly evolved through adaptive radiation into some eight hundred species unique to the islands. Among them are the Hawaiian tree snails. Many brightly colored, varied species of Achatinellids, called kāhuli, evolved in the rain forests of Hawai`i, Maui, Lāna`i, Moloka`i, and O`ahu.

Achatinella snails, called O`ahu tree snails or "little agates," live only in the forests of O`ahu. O`ahu tree snails are 1 inch (3 centimeters) long, with shells that are banded in bright colors that vary widely in pattern and design. They live in very small areas, some only as large as one tree.

Little agates become active at night or during heavy rain. They graze on fungi growing along the undersides of the leaves of trees. They eat delicately, scraping each leaf with their tiny teeth without damaging it. When the sun is out, they seal themselves up inside their colorful shells, pressed tightly against a small branch or leaf.

Unlike many mollusks, or soft-bodied invertebrates, tree snails are born alive, already housed in tiny, delicate, colorful shells that match their parents' colors and patterns. They are about 0.2 inch (5 millimeters) long at birth. They grow very slowly, taking four to five years to reach reproductive maturity.

Even as adults, tree snails move slowly, sliding along at about 3 inches (8 centimeters) a minute. An average snail produces only four or five offspring per year. Most of the offspring die from natural causes within their first year.

ABUNDANT PLANT LIFE

Most of the plant diversity of the Hawaiian rain forest thrives in its lowest level, the groundcover. More than fifty species of shade-loving ferns grow in the `Ōla`a forest. Among them are the `ama`u, which has a thick, stout trunk and can grow as tall as tree ferns; the delicate, lacey `ākōlea; and a stiff, gray-green fern called hō`i`o kula. The hardy palapalai has soft, hairy, lacy fronds. The ohaa ku and palai hina hina are smaller, filmy ferns.

Epiphytic ferns, mosses, liverworts, and tree seedlings grow in abundance in very wet forests. In Hawaiian rain forests, including `Ōla`a, soft clusters of them hang over long tree branches, draped thickly like green curtains. Several species of a large epiphyte called `ēkaha are found in `Ōla`a. The leafless moa, which has long flat branches, hangs off dead, moss-filmed logs. Mats of mosses and liverworts—about 150 different kinds—cover snags, logs, and tree branches. Many small epiphytes of the `Ōla`a—wahine noho mauna, kihi, maku`e lau li`i, and kolokolo—climb high along the branches of the forest's trees, reaching into the upper layers.

Shrubs, herbs, and saplings of the forest's canopy trees also populate the groundcover layer. `Ala`ala wai nui is a flowering plant in the black pepper family. A hydrangea plant called the pū`ahanui grows into the understory layer. Other shrubs are the tree `ōhelo and the `ilihia, a member of the African violet family.

PŪ`AHANUI (BROUSSAISIA ARGUTA)

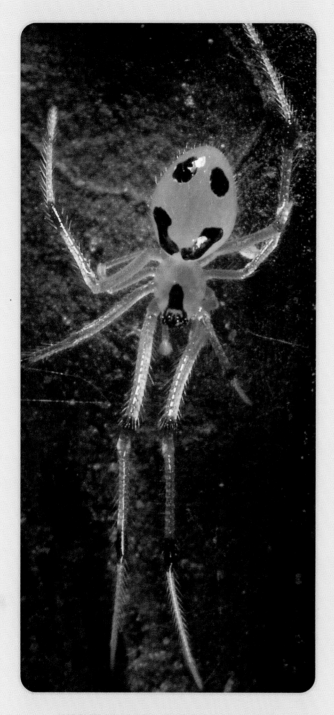

HAPPYFACE SPIDER *(THERIDION GRALLATOR)*

THE HAPPYFACE SPIDER

The happyface spider has a yellowish body with red-and-black markings on its abdomen that look like the eyes and smiling mouth of a happy face button. The spider's markings may serve as camouflage to protect it from forest birds.

Happyface spiders live on the undersides of the leaves of the pūʻahanui and other plants. When flies and other insects land on the top side of the leaf or crawl under the leaf to escape the rain, happyface spiders stalk them and catch them with a sticky rope they have woven. Female happyface spiders catch insects and feed them to their young.

CHAPTER 5
`ŌHI`A, TOP TO BOTTOM

The flexible, slow-growing `ōhi`a tree, or `ōhi`a lehua, is the most widespread native tree in the Hawaiian Islands. It is dominant or codominant in nearly every ecological zone; it dominates 80 percent of the Hawaiian rain forest. Throughout the Hawaiian Islands, the `ōhi`a feeds, waters, protects, and shelters hundreds of arthropods, birds, flowering plants, and ferns.

The `ōhi`a is extremely adaptable. It thrives at high and low elevations, both at altitudes higher than the `Ōla`a forest and near the ocean. It grows tall and straight in some areas but often, especially in windy areas, has a trunk and branches that are twisted and gnarly. Exposed to open sunlight, it can reach as high as 100 feet (30 meters). In bogs or deeply shaded areas, it grows no higher than 2 or 3 feet (less than 1 meter). It often develops epiphytically on other trees.

The `ōhi`a needs very little soil to grow and can take hold on newly formed lava.

Its height is not necessarily dependent on the richness of the soil. Some of the taller `ōhi`a trees in the Hawaiian Islands need very little soil, while in other areas where the soil is richer and deeper, `ōhi`a grow to shorter heights.

BLOSSOMING FOREST

In the `Ōla`a forest, the `ōhi`a tree grows thickly in many areas, creating a closed canopy through which little sunlight passes. The forest is shady, damp, and cool beneath the `ōhi`a canopy, which shelters the ground beneath it from the sun's heat.

`Ōhi`a blossoms (lehua) are usually red but can be yellow, pink, or orange. They grow throughout the year, but their flowering peaks twice every year, once in winter and once in summer. The flowers produce sweet nectar, food for `apapane and `i`iwi birds.

`Ōhi`a fruits are small capsules with chambers that split apart when dry.

(ABOVE) ʻŌHIʻA TREES
(METROSIDEROS POLYMORPHA)

(ABOVE LEFT) ʻŌHIʻA TREES CAN GROW IN
NEWLY COOLED LAVA.

(LEFT) AN ʻŌHIʻA BLOSSOM (LEHUA)

Tiny seeds are released, and the wind blows them to surrounding areas. The seeds take root easily, sprouting quickly to seedlings in the crevices of rocks or lava flows. If the seedlings grow in areas of high rainfall, they can become full-sized trees in twenty years. If they find homes in a deeply closed forest, they may grow epiphytically on logs or on other trees.

The `ōhi`a tree's roots reach into the soil but also twist at the base of the trunk. As the tree ages, its roots grow thick and tangled. In these matted root clusters, new `ōhi`a and other plants take root and grow.

On the floor of the rain forest, `ōhi`a snags and logs are home to many fungi, such as small mushrooms. Ferns and herbs grow epiphytically on the snags. Native birds use snags as territorial sites (places they claim as their own), nest sites, or perches. Insects lay their eggs in the bark or wood of snags and dead, fallen `ōhi`a trees.

THE CHANGING FOREST

The rain forest changes over time. Weather conditions vary from season to season, over decades, centuries, or millennia. The populations and kinds of plants and animals growing within each area of the forest change. The nature and chemistry of the soil is transformed. None of these changes occurs in a vacuum. The changes are interdependent, affecting one another.

In the `Ōla`a forest, an important phenomenon that causes and is caused by change is "`ōhi`a dieback." `Ōhi`a dieback occurs when large sections of `ōhi`a tree stands within the Hawaiian rain forest die at the same time. Such a

> **THE `ŌHI`A TREE'S ROOTS REACH INTO THE SOIL BUT ALSO TWIST AT THE BASE OF THE TRUNK. AS THE TREE AGES, ITS ROOTS GROW THICK AND TANGLED. IN THESE MATTED ROOT CLUSTERS, NEW `ŌHI`A AND OTHER PLANTS TAKE ROOT AND GROW.**

population change has a serious impact on the rain forest because the `ōhi`a is such a dominant tree. In the 1970s, extensive stands of `ōhi`a trees died. In those stands, virtually every canopy tree died. About half of the rain forest growing on the eastern slopes of Mauna Loa was affected.

This dieback might have been caused by one or more factors. Because `ōhi`a are able to grow so quickly on new lava flows, many `ōhi`a often grow together at the same pace. This creates sections within the forest in which the trees are all the same age and size. As they mature, they decline and die at about the same time, creating a sudden loss of a large section of the forest's trees. `Ōhi`a dieback also can be triggered by pathogens, organisms such as viruses or bacteria that can cause disease. Serious climate changes—like a drought, a year of unusually heavy rains, or even strong winds that topple trees—can also cause dieback.

Another possible cause of `ōhi`a dieback is a change in the soil. Soil composition can change in various ways. Younger soils have higher levels of phosphorus, an important nutrient for

A STAND OF `ŌHI`A TREES

growing plants. As soils age, plants slowly leach phosphorus from the soil. Soil can also become waterlogged from climatic changes. Different plants have different soil needs, so as soils change, the kinds of plants living in them also change. For example, `ōhi`a trees cannot grow in very wet soil.

When a stand of trees occupying a large area of the forest dies, the area becomes open rather than closed canopy, and sunlight comes through. This affects the kinds of plants that grow in the area. Sometimes the sun reaches young `ōhi`a saplings that are able to grow taller and fill the canopy, closing it again. Sometimes shade-loving ferns that have already filled the understory continue to hide `ōhi`a saplings from the sun. The saplings are unable to grow taller, and the forest remains open. Different kinds of sun-loving plants begin to grow in the area, eventually crowding out the ferns.

WHEN THE CANOPY OPENS UP DUE TO DIEBACK, DIFFERENT PLANT SPECIES BEGIN TO APPEAR IN THE RAIN FOREST. SUN-LOVING PLANTS, SUCH AS THIS PASSIONFLOWER *(PASSIFLORA SUBEROSA)*, MAY TAKE OVER WHERE `ŌHI`A TREES ONCE THRIVED.

CHAPTER 6
PEOPLE AND THE HAWAIIAN RAIN FOREST

The Hawaiian Islands began forming millions of years ago. The islands' earliest inhabitants, plants and animals, arrived soon after, one by one every one hundred thousand years or so. They evolved rapidly, populating the islands with thousands of kinds of plants and animals.

The first humans arrived hundreds of thousands of years later, sometime between A.D. 300 and 750. Polynesians from the Marquesas Islands sailed over in double-hulled canoes. They used their extensive sailing experience and knowledge of the wind, ocean currents, clouds, and sea life, as well as

> **THE HAWAIIAN ISLANDS BEGAN FORMING MILLIONS OF YEARS AGO. THE ISLANDS' EARLIEST INHABITANTS, PLANTS AND ANIMALS, ARRIVED SOON AFTER, ONE BY ONE EVERY ONE HUNDRED THOUSAND YEARS OR SO.**

the stars and the moon, to help them navigate the wide expanse of open ocean. Over the following years, more arrivals sailed among the Hawaiian Islands and other neighboring islands, bringing along plants and animals native to their homes.

The arrivals brought as many as twenty-six kinds of plants alien to the islands. Among them were bananas, sugarcane, sweet potatoes, kalo, coconuts, breadfruit, mountain apples, and various medicinal plants. They brought moa, a kind of jungle fowl; pua`a, or Polynesian pigs; and small dogs called `īlio. They brought unintended stowaways as well: rats, lizards, snails, and lice.

These early Hawaiians burned forests near the shores of the islands to clear land for farming. They set up breadfruit groves and intricate systems of terraces to plant kalo (known elsewhere as taro), a sweet root plant that would become an important part of Hawaiian cultural life. They built homes made of large rocks locked into strong walls that withstood the earthquakes that periodically shook the islands. They dammed streams to irrigate their kalo fields.

As people cleared forests for farmland, they radically altered the lowland ecosystems. Many insects and snails disappeared. The animals that had been brought to the islands easily caught and killed the flightless birds that had evolved when no predators roamed the islands. At least sixty species of birds quickly disappeared soon after the arrival of the early Hawaiians. Water birds

(ABOVE) **BREADFRUIT (*ARTOCARPUS ALTILIS*)**

(LEFT) **AN AGRICULTURAL FIELD PLANTED WITH KALO (*COLOCASIA ESCULENTA*)**

flourished in areas where they had not lived before, because damming had created new bodies of water.

The Hawaiians believed that "the rain follows the forest." They were careful to preserve the rain forests that grew midway up the mountainsides. From upland forests in elevations above the rain forests, they cut down koa trees, dragging them to the shore and using the hard, dense wood to build canoes. They quarried stone to make into adzes (cutting tools similar to axes without handles). They killed native birds for their feathers, sewing the brightly colored feathers into robes. They used `ohelo berries to make dye for their clothing.

The early Hawaiians regulated use of the rain forests through a system called kapu. The people were ruled by chiefs who controlled land division under a system that divided the islands into districts. Units within the districts incorporated mountain peaks and surrounding lands seaward, so that each unit contained every major ecological resource zone.

Hawaiians worshiped various gods, including Pele, the goddess of volcanoes. Pele was believed to have lived on various

`ŌHELO *(VACCINIUM RETICULATUM)* BERRIES

islands, moving from one to the next and creating volcanic activities wherever she went. On Hawai`i, her most recent home, she dug out two places to live: Mauna Loa and—her favorite residence—Mauna Kīlauea. Hawaiians believe she is still pushing lava out of the mountain's vents in periodic volcanic eruptions.

Pigs were, and still are, important in Hawaiian culture. They were used as food, as rent payments to chiefs, and as sacrificial animals in religious ceremonies. Pigs were offered in praise to Lōno, the great god of plants and planting. Before a new canoe was launched, pigs were cooked in underground ovens and offered to Kāne, protector of sea travelers. If a cooked pig's skin was unwrinkled, the trip would go smoothly. If the skin was cracked, the canoe trip could be disastrous. Young pigs ran loose, but they stayed near the homes of people and away from the forest. Older pigs were put into pens and fattened with scraps of sweet potatoes, breadfruit, and bananas. Women and children were not allowed to eat pigs. Following coming-of-age ceremonies, boys could eat pigs alongside other men.

MAUNA KĪLAUEA IS CONSIDERED BY NATIVE HAWAIIANS TO BE THE GODDESS PELE'S FAVORED HOME.

The hard wood of koa trees was used to build canoes, bowls, spears, and house supports. In their search for trees to be cut, woodworkers followed `elepaio birds flitting through the koa forests. When a bird landed near a koa and gave its call, workers took it as a sign that the tree was a good selection. Following ceremonies honoring Ku, the god of building, they cut down the tree.

EUROPEAN ARRIVALS

In 1778 Captain James Cook became the first European to reach the Hawaiian Islands.

In this and subsequent journeys, his crew brought geese, goats, cats, ducks, sheep, and new vegetables such as pumpkins, melons, and onions to the islands. In the lower decks, more stowaways arrived: tapeworms, flatworms, fleas, flies, scorpions, centipedes, earthworms, and roaches.

One of Cook's most significant contributions—which would quickly create a serious danger to the islands' delicate ecosystems—was the modern pig. The European sows and boars he brought to the islands bred with the smaller Hawaiian pigs, and their offspring evolved into feral,

CAPTAIN JAMES COOK (THIRD FROM RIGHT IN SECOND ROW) **MEETS WITH HAWAIIAN NATIVES.**

or wild, pigs. About one hundred thousand of these pigs still wander the islands. Four thousand of them live in Hawai`i Volcanoes National Park.

In the first half of the 1800s, more than eight thousand alien plants and animals were introduced. Silkworms and honeybees were imported to produce silk and honey. Game birds and rabbits were brought in for the growing European population to hunt for sport.

The introduced plants and animals played havoc with the delicate ecosystems of the Hawaiian Islands, including the forests. New plant and animal species crowded out native and endemic species. Banana poke and guava choked out native vines and plants. Cats killed native birds. Rats ate birds' eggs. Pigs and cattle destroyed habitat, eating ferns, lobelioids like `ōhā, and other understory plants, and digging up the ground. Plants and animals needing damp shade—like lobelioids, tree snails, and many native birds—were pushed farther and farther into the higher-elevation forests. By the mid-1800s, most of the native species of the lowlands had been eradicated.

(ABOVE) **GUAVA (PSIDIUM) GROVES AND OTHER AGRICULTURAL FIELDS HAVE REPLACED MUCH OF THE HAWAIIAN ISLANDS' NATURAL WILDERNESS.**

(RIGHT) **BANANA POKE (PASSIFLORA MOLLISSIMA)**

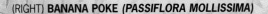

FERAL PIGS *(Sus scrofa)*

Feral pigs caused—and continue to cause—tremendous damage to Hawaiian ecosystems. Pigs graze on almost any plant life. They burrow into the ground to dig up enormous amounts of vegetation. They can weigh as much as 400 to 500 pounds (about 200 kilograms), and are strong enough to push aside boulders.

The plants of the rain forest—which have lost the thorns, poisons, and offensive scents that protect plants in other parts of the world—are defenseless against these aggressive animals. The plants' shallow root systems, important aids in clinging to the barest rock or thinnest soils, are easy to dig up and destroy. Pigs move through the forest like living tractors, turning over great chunks of soil. They devour delicate ferns, saplings, and other plants of the groundcover and understory. Their rooting also exposes the soil to erosion.

As they turn up soil, pigs create holes that fill with water and become muddy, stagnant puddles—ideal breeding grounds

FERAL PIGS ARE VERY SPEEDY AND RARELY STILL. THIS PIG WAS CAUGHT IN ACTION, SCURRYING THROUGH A FIELD.

for mosquitoes and other alien insects. Pigs also push down tall hāpu`u pulu ferns, ripping them open to eat the inner pith (the soft, spongy interior of the stem) and leaving empty husks that capture rainwater and also attract alien insects. Mosquitoes carry bacteria that can cause diseases, including avian malaria. This disease infects and kills native forest birds, which never developed immunity against such diseases because no carriers of the disease existed on the islands until mosquitoes arrived.

HĀPU`U PULU FERNS

Moving from one area to the next, pigs carry seeds caught in their feet. They inadvertently plant species in new areas and change the composition of ecosystems. When foraging pigs devour overhanging ferns, entire sections of the forest open up to the sun. Where shade-loving plants native to the rain forest once grew, new alien grasses and other sun-loving plants take over. These aggressive plants crowd out the native plants. The entire ecosystem is altered.

Scientists want to eradicate pigs from the rain forest. But pigs continue to be important in Hawaiian culture. Conflicts arise between native Hawaiians who want to retain their cultural identity and scientists who are trying to preserve the imperiled forests. One compromise has been to remove pigs from certain target areas of the forest, while allowing hunting to continue in other places. Scientists and Hawaiian natives continue to seek compromises in their conflicting views of how best to care for the Hawaiian forests.

Cook's party also brought European diseases, against which Hawai`i's human population had no defenses. People develop immunities to viruses when they are exposed to them over time. But such diseases as gonorrhea, syphilis, and cholera had never existed on the Hawaiian Islands. In 1804 a cholera epidemic killed thousands of Hawaiians. Gonorrhea rendered Hawaiian women infertile, further reducing the native population. The islands' human population had dropped from between four hundred thousand and one million in 1778 to seventy-two thousand by 1853.

In 1848 control of the land was moved away from chiefs and into private ownership by nonnative occupants. Plantations flourished, growing sugarcane, coffee beans, and rice. Immigrants were brought in from other countries to work on the plantations, and they brought more plants and animals from their varied homelands.

By the early 1900s, so much natural forest had been cut and destroyed that concerns about availability of water for

EARLY HAWAIIAN SUGARCANE PLANTATION

NORFOLK PINE *(ARAUCARIA HETEROPHYLLA)*

drinking and irrigation led to government programs to reforest the islands. But officials used quick-growing foreign species, like eucalyptus and Norfolk pine, rather than slow-growing native trees, like `ōhi`a. New plants and animals, imported to address problems, instead created new ones. For example, blackberries were imported to feed the game birds that had been brought for sport. But they crowded out native plants. The mongoose, which had been imported to kill rats, instead killed ground-nesting native birds.

A DELICATE FUTURE

Hawaiian rain forests are the most imperiled of all rain forests. Almost half of the original forested acreage has been lost. The Hawaiian Islands have been called "the endangered species capital of the world." About one-third of all the world's endangered species of birds and plants live in Hawaiian rain forests. Almost 80 percent of the original birds of the Hawaiian rain forest have become extinct since the arrival of people. Of more than 150 kinds of forest birds that were endemic to the

Hawaiian Islands, thirty-nine species remain. Many are endangered, and some are represented by only ten to twenty individual birds. Among the honeycreeper species alone, only twenty-six of the dozens that evolved on the islands remain, and sixteen of them are endangered.

In the early 1900s, the United States established a national park system to help preserve important areas. In 1916 Hawai`i Volcanoes National Park was established. Mauna Kīlauea and Mauna Loa were the first areas to be protected.

Efforts to save what is left of the Hawaiian rain forest will succeed or fail in the next decade. Many strategies are showing promise. The greatest damage to the forest has been due to the introduction of alien species. Scientists have battled pig destruction by building fences around targeted rain forest areas, keeping the destructive animals out. They capture them with snares and traps or systematically hunt and kill them.

Removing invasive plants has been more difficult because so many species have been introduced, and they are easily and widely dispersed.

Koa trees are susceptible to severe damage from grazing animals like goats and cattle. Koas have regenerated well in places where these animals have been removed. The koa is one of the few native rain forest trees that responds well to fire—it seems to stimulate koa root growth and seed germination. Areas in the `Ōla`a forest where koa had once burned down have young koa groves, sometimes near older surviving trees or tree stumps. Because the koa is a fast-growing tree, scientists are looking to sustainable koa forestry as a promising tool in rebuilding and preserving Hawaiian rain forests.

Scientists are not the only people who can help save the Hawaiian forests. Through responsible stewardship, everyone can take steps to help preserve the resources of the earth, including its forests.

`ŌLA`A RAIN FOREST

WHAT YOU CAN DO

If you visit the Hawaiian Islands, don't bring plants, fruits, vegetables, or animals along. Seeds, insects, and diseases can hitchhike a ride and then establish themselves in the islands. Leave pets at home. Rabbits detroy vegetation, cats kill native birds, and even acquarium fish released into streams compete with native inhabitants.

If you're hiking or camping in the Hawaiian Islands, stay on the trail. Don't trample fragile undergrowth. Don't pick flowers or keep wild creatures for pets. Leave plants and animals where you find them.

Before entering the forest, clean your hiking boots, shoes, and other gear. If you don't do this, alien weeds can travel along with you. They may grow in habitats that cannot accommodate them.

Watch for foreign plants and animals. Report snakes, alligators, parrots, banana poke, or other exotics to the State Department of Agriculture, (808) 548-0844 or (808) 586-PEST.

If your family has a sailboat, help to keep it clean. Ballast water can carry foreign algae, mollusks, and other harmful species. Don't bring potted plants or other living material to the Hawaiian Islands on your boat. They can carry larvae of alien insects.

Don't order Hawaiian plants through the mail. Ask your friends not to mail plants to you.

TAKE CARE OF YOUR OWN "HAWAIIAN RAIN FOREST"

Wherever you live, your community has its own ecosystem, where plants, animals, and insects coexist with the area's climate, soil, and water. Learn about what's growing in your own backyard. Are there any endangered species in your state? What are their predators?

What's growing in your home garden? Learn which species of plants are native to your part of the country. Choose from these when deciding what to plant in your garden. Nonnative plants can be pretty but might also spread and crowd out native varieties.

Do you have cats? Keep them inside. Cats are one of the most serious threats to urban wildlife, especially birds.

When hiking or visiting nature reserves and parks, stay on the trail. Don't trample or pick the vegetation. Leave fallen bark, twigs, and branches on the ground where they have fallen.

REDUCE, REUSE, RECYCLE

Reduce paper use. Use both sides of each piece of paper in your notebook. Use cloth napkins and towels. Avoid using disposable paper plates and cups. Look for tree-free paper, which is made from agricultural products like waste straw, kenaf (hibiscus fibers), and hemp. Avoid disposable containers. But if you must choose between paper or plastic, choose paper—it breaks down more easily.

Reduce your use of gasoline and plastic. They are made from petroleum, or oil. Some oil is extracted from rain forests and harms the forests. Ride your bike or take a bus whenever you can.

Reduce packaging. Try not to buy products packaged in extra materials, such as styrofoam.

Reduce your red meat consumption. Millions of acres of rain forest are cleared into pastures for cows that are made into hamburgers and other meat products. When ordering at restaurants, choose foods that are beef-free. Ask your parents to help you list healthy, beef-free foods to eat at home.

Reduce your use of water and electricity. Don't leave water running when you're not using it. Use mulch to conserve water in your garden. Turn down the heat in your home, and wear a sweater. Lower your thermostat by one degree per hour for every hour you'll be away or asleep.

Reuse items at home. Use empty paper bags or pet food bags to line your trash cans instead of plastic liners. Use scrap paper for notes and messages. Reuse bread bags and margarine tubs. Store foods and drinks in reusable containers and bottles. Instead of throwing away clothing or household items that you no longer want, take them to a thrift shop.

Recycle food and plants by starting a compost pile. Add nonmeat and nondairy food scraps, as well as yard and garden trimmings, to the pile.

Recycle gardening and household products. Take extra plastic or rubber pots back to the nursery. Recycle newspapers, cans, glass bottles and jars, aluminum foil, and motor oil.

GET ACTIVE

Be a good example. Your own behavior will encourage your family, friends, and neighbors. Join a conservation organization. Volunteer your time to conservation projects. Volunteer for tree-planting projects with your school, church, or civic club.

Write letters to your senator or representative. Be specific. State the problem and what you would like done to address it. Keep in touch, so your representative knows this is important to you. Letters have helped bring about important laws, such as the Endangered Species Act of 1973.

To write to senators from your state:
The Honorable (name of your senator)
United States Senate
Washington, DC 20510

To write to your representative in Congress:
The Honorable (name of your representative)
U.S. House of Representatives
Washington, DC 20510

WEBSITES TO VISIT FOR MORE INFORMATION

Conservation International (CI)

<http://www.conservation.org>
Conservation International's mission is to conserve the earth's biodiversity and to demonstrate that humans can live harmoniously with nature. Its website contains conservation news and information about CI's programs.

Greenpeace

<http://www.greenpeace.org>
Greenpeace is an organization that exposes global environmental problems. Its website contains information about a variety of environmental issues, including protecting the world's ancient forests.

The Nature Conservancy of Hawai`i

<http://nature.org/wherewework /northamerica/states/hawaii/about/>
The Nature Conservancy is an international organization that preserves the diversity of life by protecting the lands and waters. The Nature Conservancy of Hawai`i has protected more than 200,000 acres (80,000 hectares) of Hawaiian natural areas that shelter native species.

Rainforest Action Network (RAN)

<http://www.ran.org>
<http://www.rainforestweb.org>
The Rainforest Action Network works to protect tropical rain forests and the people living in and around them. Their website contains news about rain forest issues, information about RAN projects, and a Kid's Corner with activities, videos, and more. Rainforestweb.org is RAN's World Rainforest Information Portal, with links to a wide variety of rain forest information and resources.

World Resources Institute (WRI)

<http://www.wri.org>
The World Resources Institute is an environmental think tank that works to find practical ways to protect the earth and improve people's lives. EarthTrends, WRI's Environmental Information Portal, provides links to information on a wide variety of environmental topics.

FURTHER READING

Fredericks, Anthony D. *Exploring the Rainforest: Science Activities for Kids*. Golden, CO: Fulcrum Publishing, 1996.

Hickman, Pamela. *In the Woods*. Halifax, Nova Scotia: Formac Publishing Company Ltd., 1998.

Kittinger, Jo S. *Dead Log Alive!* New York: Franklin Watts, 1996.

Lasky, Kathryn. *The Most Beautiful Roof in the World: Exploring the Rainforest Canopy*. New York: Harcourt Brace & Co., 1997.

Leuzzi, Linda. *Life Connections: Pioneers in Ecology*. New York: Franklin Watts, 2000.

Massa, Renato. *The Tropical Forest*. Austin, TX: Raintree Steck-Vaughn, 1997.

McClung, Robert M. *Lost Wild America: The Story of Our Extinct and Vanishing Wildlife*. Hamden, CT: Linnet Books, 1993.

Orr, Richard. *Nature Cross-Sections*. New York: DK Publishing, Inc., 1995.

Patent, Dorothy Hinshaw. *Biodiversity*. New York: Clarion Books, 1996.

Russo, Monica. *The Tree Almanac: A Year-Round Activity Guide*. New York: Sterling Publishing Company, 1993.

Sayre, April Pulley. *Tropical Rain Forest*. New York: Twenty-First Century Books, 1994.

Scott, Michael. *Ecology*. New York: Oxford University Press, 1995.

Staub, Frank. *America's Forests*. Minneapolis, MN: Carolrhoda Books, 1999.

VanCleave, Janice. *Ecology for Every Kid: Easy Activities that Make Learning About Science Fun*. New York: John Wiley & Sons, 1996.

Walker, Sally M. *Water Up, Water Down: The Hydrologic Cycle*. Minneapolis, MN: Carolrhoda Books, 1992.

Whitman, Sylvia. *This Land Is Your Land*. Minneapolis, MN: Lerner Publications Company, 1994.

GLOSSARY

A note on pronunciation of Hawaiian words: Consonants are pronounced as in English. Vowels are pronounced *a* as in *above*, *e* as in *bet*, *i* as in *machine*, *o* as in *sole*, and *u* as in *rule*. The kahakō (a horizontal line over a vowel) indicates that the vowel sound is elongated. The `okina (a single left quote) indicates a break in the breath, as in "oh-oh!"

adaptive radiation: the evolution of one species into many new species

archipelago: a chain of islands

arthropod: an animal that has a segmented body, jointed legs, and a hard outer skeleton instead of bones

canopy: the top layer of a forest, made up of the branches of the tallest trees

colonizer: a plant or animal that finds its way from the mainland to an island and becomes established there

deciduous: losing leaves in the fall and growing new ones in the spring

decomposer: an organism that breaks down dead plants and animals into nutrients that can be used by plants

diversity: the number of different species living in an ecosystem

dominant species: the species that is most common within an ecosystem or has the most influence on the ecosystem

ecosystem: a community of plants and animals, along with their environment

emergent trees: tall trees that poke up above a forest's canopy

endemic: living in only one particular area

epiphyte: a plant that grows on another plant but gets the moisture and nutrients it needs from the air and rain; an "air plant"

evolution: the process by which plant and animal species change over time

groundcover: the bottom layer of a forest, including soil, forest litter, and the smallest plants

habitat: the kind of environment in which a species normally lives

honeycreeper: any of about forty species of birds endemic to the Hawaiian Islands

hot spot: a weak spot in one of the plates making up the earth's crust

humus: rich soil particles produced by the decay of plant and animal matter

invertebrate: an animal that has no backbone

keystone species: any species that is critical to the survival of other species living within its ecosystem

kīpuka: an older section of lava on which vegetation has grown

larva (pl. larvae): an insect in an early stage of its development

lava: molten rock coming out of a volcano, or such rock that has cooled and hardened

lichen: a "double plant" consisting of an alga growing inside a fungus

magma: molten rock found within the earth

mantle: the part of the interior of the earth between the central core and the crust

mollusk: a soft-bodied invertebrate, such as a tree snail

photosynthesis: the process by which green plants use sunlight, carbon dioxide, and water to make their own food

pollinate: to transfer pollen from one flower to another so seeds can form

primary consumer: a plant-eating animal; an herbivore

primary producer: a plant or other organism that makes its own food

rain forest: a forest made up of tall trees growing close together in an area that receives more than 100 inches (250 centimeters) of rainfall per year

secondary consumer: an animal that eats other animals; a carnivore or predator

snag: a standing dead tree

speciation: the process by which an organism's traits change so much that it becomes a new, separate species

species: a group of animals or plants that share common traits

trade wind: a wind blowing almost constantly in one direction

understory: the middle layer of the Hawaiian rain forest, made up of large shrubs, midsized trees, and tree ferns

windward: the side or direction from which the wind is blowing

INDEX

ABOUT THE AUTHOR

Anne Welsbacher writes science books, articles, and website content on animals, the environment, health, and medicine. She has written books for young readers on cougars, wading birds, Komodo dragons, crocodiles, pelicans, whales, sharks, and other animals, as well as on simple machines and other science topics. She also writes novels, plays, and science and history scripts for museum and other educational environments. In addition to researching and writing about nature and history, Anne enjoys running, yoga, music, hiking, and reading. She also enjoys learning about the birds and plants of her southern California neighborhood and exploring the land and marine life of the California coast. She lived near the Mississippi River in Minneapolis, Minnesota, before moving to Santa Monica, California, near the Pacific Ocean, where she lives with companion Corey Swertfager, two cats, and assorted fish and snails.

PHOTO ACKNOWLEDGEMENTS

The photographs in this book are reproduced courtesy of, © Douglas Peebles/CORBIS, pp. 2–3; PhotoDisc (Royalty Free), border; © Pacific Pictures/John Penisten, pp. 7, 8, 15, 17 (right), 53 (left), 54; Maps and diagrams by Bill Hauser, pp. 10, 12, 22; © Paul Buklarewicz, pp. 11, 25, 28, 29 (both), 30, 31 (top), 33, 35 (both), 36 (both), 42, 43 (both), 45, 48 (top left and right), 50, 53 (right), 55, 57 (both), 58, 59, 61, 63; © Kay Shaw Photography, pp. 14, 48 (bottom left); © Dave Fleetham/Visuals Unlimited, p. 16; © Tim Davis/Photo Researchers, pp. 17 (left), 20; © Jack Jeffrey, p. 18; © Photo Researchers, p. 19; © Kjell B. Sandved, p. 31 (bottom); © William P. Mull, p. 37; © S. L. Montgomery, pp. 38, 46; Hawaii Biological Survey, p. 40; © Gregory G. Dimijian, M.D./Photo Researchers, p. 44; © Douglas Peebles, p. 51; Library of Congress, p. 56; Hawaii State Archives, p. 60. Cover: © Douglas Peebles/CORBIS.